I AM
AMAZING

Dr. Katherine Y. Brown

www.TrueVinePublishing.org

I Am Amazing
Dr. Katherine Y. Brown

Published by True Vine Publishing Co.
810 Dominican Dr.
Nashville, TN 37228
www.TrueVinePublishing.org

Copyright © 2023 by Dr. Katherine Y. Brown
All rights reserved. No part of this book may be reproduced in any form or by any electronic or mechanical means, including information storage and retrieval or mechanical means without permission in writing from the publisher, except by a reviewer who may quote brief passages in a review.

ISBN: 978-1-962783-88-0 Paperback
ISBN 978-1-962783-08-8 eBook

Printed in the United States of America—First printing

DEDICATION

This book is dedicated to the courageous who dare to remember their own amazingness, even when the world attempts to dim their light. To those who will rediscover just how wonderful they truly are through these pages, and to anyone who, even for a moment, questions their worth. Let there be no doubt: you are amazing. Keep shining, keep striving, and keep embracing the inner you – for you are, and always will be, **amazing**.

Are you hiding your greatness because you're scared or worried about what others might think? That's not good. Everyone can be a leader in their own way. Sometimes, they just don't know it yet.

To really see your worth and share it with others, you might need to think a bit differently. It's a change, but it's one we can make. And it starts with us. I'm ready to take on this challenge. And I hope, after reading this, you will be too.

CHAPTER 1:
UNDERSTANDING YOUR AMAZING SELF

There are many things that make each one of us special. Sometimes, though, we don't share these unique traits with the world because we are afraid to be different or stand out. But being different isn't something to be afraid of — it's something to celebrate. In this book, we're going to explore some very important words that can help you understand just how amazing you are.

These words are...

SPECIAL

When we say something is special, we mean it's not common or ordinary. It's unique and has its own kind of magic. You are special because there's no one else in the entire world who's just like you!

> **JUST LIKE A SNOWFLAKE, YOU'RE SPECIAL. NO TWO OF US ARE THE SAME. EMBRACE YOUR UNIQUENESS.**

COURAGE

Courage isn't about being fearless; it's about being brave even when you're scared. It's the voice inside you that says, "I can do this," even when a task seems difficult. Just like a superhero using their superpowers to save the day, your courage is your superpower to face any challenge.

> **COURAGE ISN'T THE ABSENCE OF FEAR, IT'S THE DECISION TO TAKE A STEP EVEN WHEN YOU'RE AFRAID.**

RESILIENCE

Resilience is like a rubber band. Even when it's stretched to its limit, a rubber band always bounces back to its original shape. Similarly, resilience is your ability to bounce back from tough times, learn from them, and become even stronger.

> YOU NEVER KNOW HOW FAR YOU CAN STRETCH UNTIL YOU TRY. BE LIKE A RUBBER BAND, ALWAYS BOUNCE BACK AND SHOW YOUR RESILIENCE.

SELF-EMPOWERMENT

It means taking control of our own lives, making positive choices, and believing in our ability to make things happen. It's like being the captain of your own ship, steering your life in the direction you want to go.

> **SELF-EMPOWERMENT IS MORE THAN WHAT WE SAY, IT'S WHAT WE DO. REMEMBER, YOU ARE THE CAPTAIN OF YOUR SHIP; NAVIGATE TOWARDS YOUR DREAMS.**

SELF-ESTEEM

This is a word about recognizing your worth and being proud of who you are. It's like seeing yourself in a mirror and saying, "I am special. I am capable. I am amazing."

> **YOUR SELF-ESTEEM MATTERS.
> LOOK IN THE MIRROR, SAY IT
> LOUD AND CLEAR:
> I AM SPECIAL, I AM CAPABLE,
> I AM AMAZING.**

INSPIRE

To inspire means to fill someone with the urge or ability to do or feel something, especially to do something creative. It's about stirring up positive feelings and actions in ourselves and others. No matter who you are or where you come from, your story, your truth, can inspire those around you and even the world!

> **SHARING YOUR TRUTH CAN INSPIRE THE WORLD. YOUR VOICE MATTERS.**

HOPE

Hope is like a small light in a dark room. Even when things seem hard or impossible, hope keeps us going, guiding us towards better times. It's about looking forward to brighter days no matter how dark it seems at the moment.

> EVEN IN THE DARKEST TIMES, HOPE CAN ILLUMINATE YOUR PATH. KEEP BELIEVING IN BRIGHTER DAYS.

FAITH

Faith is another powerful word. Faith is trusting in something, even when you can't see it. It's about believing in the goodness of the world, in the kindness of others, and in your own abilities, even when things are difficult.

> FAITH IS THE BIRD THAT FEELS THE LIGHT EVEN WHEN THE DAWN IS STILL DARK. TRUST IN YOUR JOURNEY.

BELIEVE

To believe is to have confidence in the truth, the existence, or the reliability of something, even without absolute proof that it's possible. It's about believing in yourself, your dreams, and your abilities.

> **BELIEVE IN YOURSELF, EVEN WHEN OTHERS DOUBT. YOUR BELIEF IS YOUR POWER.**

These words are more than just definitions in a dictionary; they're keys to understanding your amazing self. As you turn the pages of this book, you will see these words come to life through the story of a young girl named Roberta. Roberta was a lot like you might be or maybe even like someone you know–she didn't realize how <u>amazing</u> she was until she understood the meaning of these words.

It's time for you to explore what makes you special, just like she did. This is a journey of self-discovery, courage, resilience, hope, faith, and belief. Because no matter where we are from, no matter who we are, there's one thing we all have in common: we are all amazing.

Journal

CHAPTER 2:
THE AMAZING ROBERTA

Once upon a time, in a small village, there lived a girl named Roberta. She led a simple life, filled with daily tasks such as helping her family cook, clean, and care for the animals. She also attended a small school in her village. Everyone around her saw her as just another girl. Even Roberta herself didn't realize her own amazingness.

One day, Roberta's teacher gave her an unusual homework assignment. She was asked to list twenty-one things that made her amazing.

When the assignment was given to her, she did not know she would be featured in the school talent show. Confused and unsure, Roberta took the assignment home, not knowing where to start. She was very afraid. She wondered why she had been given this assignment and could not imagine that she had something to share that anyone would want to listen to.

After a while of sitting quietly she decided to try, which took a lot of courage. That evening, she found a book tucked away in the corner of her small room. The book was filled with words like self-empowerment, self-esteem, courage, resilience, inspire, hope, faith, and believe. She began to read, hoping it might help with her assignment.

As she read, Roberta began to understand the importance and power within these words. The word special, she learned, meant being one-of-a-kind, unique, like a single snowflake in a winter storm. "Just like a snowflake, no two of us are the same. Embrace your uniqueness," she whispered as she read the book out loud to herself. Roberta felt a warm glow inside; she started to realize that she was special, too.

The word courage also ignited something inside her. She learned from reading the book that having courage was like having a superpower that allowed you to do challenging things, even when afraid. "Courage isn't the absence of fear; it's the decision to take a step even when you're afraid," she read out loud. Roberta felt brave; she realized that she actually had courage inside of her.

As she turned the pages, Roberta discovered resilience. The book described it as a rubber band that can stretch and stretch but always springs back. "You never know how far you can stretch until you try. Be like a rubber band. Always bounce back," she read. Roberta nodded, feeling her own resilience inside her.

Reading on, she discovered self-empowerment and self-esteem, words that meant she had control over her life and should feel good about herself. "You are the captain of your ship; navigate towards your dreams. Look in the mirror, say it loud and clear: 'I am special, I am capable, I am amazing,'" she read. With each word, Roberta felt more powerful and more confident.

Roberta then read the word inspire. It meant she could stir up positive feelings and actions in herself and others. "Sharing your truth can inspire the world. Your voice matters," she read, realizing she too had the power to inspire.

The last three words she read were hope, faith, and believe. These words were powerful, reminding her to keep looking forward, trusting in her journey, and having confidence in herself. "Even in the darkest times, hope can illuminate your path. Keep believing in brighter days. Faith is the bird that feels the light even when the dawn is still dark. Trust in your journey. Believe in yourself, even when others doubt. Your belief is your power," she read. Roberta felt hopeful, faithful, and believed in herself more than ever.

After closing the book, Roberta felt a new excitement within herself. She was ready to share her amazing self with her village. Nervously, she prepared for the school talent show. She started with practicing her tone, volume, cadence, and body language all of which she had learned from another book. She was ready and prepared. As she stepped onto the stage, she took a deep breath, remembering the word courage.

With newfound confidence, she began to list the twenty-one things that made her amazing. "I am a person, and I am amazing. I have a beautiful smile, and I am amazing." With each sentence, her voice grew stronger, and her smile wider. She believed in herself and the words that she spoke.

The villagers sat in awe. They hadn't realized the talent Roberta possessed. They discovered she could draw, sing, dance, design things, and so much more. As Roberta continued to share, they began to smile, cheer, and even clap. They celebrated not just her talents, but also her courage, resilience, and all the amazingness she held within.

That day changed Roberta's life, and it also changed the villagers' perspectives. Roberta learned to stand tall, to speak her truth, and to share her amazing self with the world. Because she, **just like you**, was truly amazing.

And remember, you never know what you can do until you try.

Journal

CHAPTER 3:
YOUR TURN TO SHINE

Just as Roberta had her moment to shine, now it's your turn. Yes, you! This chapter is a special challenge, just for you. Do you remember the homework Roberta was given by her teacher? It's your turn now to write down twenty-one things that make you amazing.

Maybe you're wondering, "What makes me amazing?" Remember those special words Roberta learned from her book? Special, courage, resilience, self-empowerment, self-esteem, inspire, hope, faith, and believe. These are not just words. They are like seeds that have been planted, ready to grow in your heart.

Do you believe that you are special? Just think of one thing that makes you different from anyone else. That's special! Remember: "Just like a snowflake, no two of us are the same. Embrace your uniqueness."

Have you ever done something even when you were scared? That's courage! Remember: "Courage isn't the absence of fear; it's the decision to take a step even when you're afraid."

Have you ever made a mistake and then tried again? That's resilience! Remember: "You never know how far you can stretch until you try. Be like a rubber band, always bounce back."

Do you make choices and take actions that are what's best for you? That's self-empowerment! And when you feel good about who you are, that's self-esteem! Remember: "You are the captain of your ship; navigate towards your dreams."

Have you ever done or said something that lifted someone else's spirits? That's inspiring! Remember: "Sharing your truth can inspire the world. Your voice matters."

Are you hopeful for the future? Do you have faith that things will get better? Do you believe in yourself? Remember: "Even in the darkest times, hope can illuminate your path. Keep believing in brighter days. Faith is the bird that feels the light even when the dawn is still dark. Trust in your journey. Believe in yourself, even when others doubt. Your belief is your power."

Just by reading this book, you've shown that you're an amazing person. You are curious, brave, and willing to learn. Just like Roberta, you have many wonderful qualities and talents. It's time to recognize and celebrate them.

Write down twenty-one things that make you amazing. It could be your love for animals, your ability to make people laugh, your kindness, your determination, your creativity, your ability to assemble things, your ability to write poetry, your ability to ride a bike or anything else you can think of. After each one, say out loud with animation and emotion "I am amazing" just like Roberta did.

You were created for a purpose, and you are an essential part of this world. The world is waiting on you. Yes, you, as you are reading this you must realize that you are amazing. Here are twenty-one reasons why I believe you are amazing:

You are brave.
You are kind.
You are unique.
You are a learner.
You are a dreamer.
You are a doer.
You are a believer.
You are a giver.
You are a fighter.
You are hopeful.
You are patient.
You are creative.
You are resilient.
You are respectful.
You are humble.
You are a friend.
You are helpful.
You are thoughtful.
You are honest.
You are loved.
You are amazing!

I Am Amazing!

Remember, you never know what you can do until you try. Write down 21 characteristics that make you amazing.

1. _____
2. _____
3. _____
4. _____
5. _____
6. _____
7. _____
8. _____
9. _____
10. _____
11. _____
12. _____
13. _____
14. _____
15. _____
16. _____
17. _____
18. _____

19._____
20._____
21._____

Journal

CHAPTER 4: SHARE THE AMAZINGNESS

You've done a wonderful job of discovering your own amazingness, and now it's time to let that light shine for others to see! Just like Roberta, who stood on that stage, shared her story, and used her courage, resilience, and self-empowerment to inspire her entire village, you too have a powerful story to share.

Remember your list of twenty-one amazing things about you? That's your story. That's your truth. And it's time to share it. Gather your friends, family, or classmates, and read this book to them. Then proudly share your list of twenty-one amazing things about you. Be loud and clear, just like Roberta, and say "I am amazing" after each point.

I Am Amazing!

_____ and I am amazing.

_____ and I am amazing.

_____ and I am amazing.

_____ and I am amazing.

_____ and I am amazing.

_____ and I am amazing.

_____ and I am amazing.

_____ and I am amazing.

_____ and I am amazing.

_____ and I am amazing.

_____ and I am amazing.

_____ and I am amazing.

_____ and I am amazing.

_____ and I am amazing.

_____ and I am amazing.

_____ and I am amazing.

_____ and I am amazing.

_____ and I am amazing.

_____ and I am amazing.

_____ and I am amazing.

At first, repeating the words "I am amazing" might seem strange. However, you truly are amazing, and it's essential for these words to become a positive affirmation in your life. You must become comfortable with affirming your greatness. Without reminders, there is a risk of forgetting your own worth and the wonderful qualities you possess.

But don't stop there. You can empower other people. Encourage your listeners, the people that you share your story with, to explore their own amazingness. Explore the words special, courage, resilience, self-empowerment, self-esteem, inspire, hope, faith, and believe with them. Share with them how each of these words can apply to their lives and empower them to create their own list of twenty-one amazing things.

Here are some suggestions on how

you can further share this book and be an inspiration to others:

- Read this book with a book club. Read it together, share your amazing qualities, and discuss Roberta's journey and what you all have learned from it.
- Volunteer to read this book at your local community center or library, and leave at least three copies of this book behind for others to discover. Encourage people to share this book with others once they're done reading.
- Post this book on social media. Share some of the twenty-one amazing things about you and encourage others to join you in celebrating their own amazingness.
- Start a creative project or make artwork based on your list of twenty-one amazing things and share it with your

school or community to showcase how you're putting this book's teachings into practice.

- Give a copy of this book to three of your friends for their birthdays. Write a special message inside the book that reminds them that they, just like you, are amazing gifts to the world.
- Pass on a copy of this book to someone who may need a little inspiration. Write your list of twenty-one amazing things about yourself on a piece of paper, place it inside the book, and encourage the person to whom you're giving the book to read your list, create their own, and then pass the book along to someone else. In this way, the book becomes a chain of inspiration, spreading from person to person, filling each reader with a sense of their own unique amazingness.

After sharing this book, have a discussion. Talk about the book, the story of Roberta, the special words, and your list of twenty-one amazing things. Ask others how they feel after reading the book or hearing your story. Discuss other ways you can all continue to spread this important message of empowerment, self-love, and resilience.

Remember, just like Roberta, you have the power to inspire others. Your story could be the spark that helps someone else realize their own amazingness. It's not just about reading a book; it's about spreading a message of hope, faith, and belief in oneself. By sharing this book, your story, and your voice, you are making a difference.

> **SHARING YOUR TRUTH CAN INSPIRE THE WORLD. YOUR VOICE MATTERS.**

I Am Amazing!

Journal

CHAPTER 5:
BELIEVE IN YOUR AMAZINGNESS - SAY IT LOUD AND PROUD!

You have started something wonderful. This is an incredible journey, discovering what makes you special, learning about your strengths, and recognizing that you, just like Roberta, are truly amazing. You've embraced important words such as special, courage, resilience, self-empowerment, self-esteem, inspire, hope, faith, and believe. You've learned what they mean, and more importantly, you've seen how they manifest in your own life. You've written down, shared, and celebrated the twenty-one amazing things about you.

Now, this is where the real excitement begins.

Don't just write down these words. Own them. Every day, say them out loud with pride and conviction. Stand tall in front of the mirror, look yourself in the eye, and declare, I am amazing!

You can even scream these words loudly if you want. The point is that you must say the words. Say it until you believe it. Say it until you glow with confidence. Say it until every corner of your being knows the reality of your amazingness.

And always believe it because it is the truth.

YOU ARE AMAZING !

Remember, no one else in this world is exactly like you. Your uniqueness, your individuality, your journey makes you special. Your courage to face life's challenges makes you strong. Your resilience to bounce back makes you unbreakable. Your self-empowerment and self-esteem make you unstoppable. And your ability to inspire, to hope, to have faith, and to believe makes you truly amazing.

YOU ARE AMAZING!

Each time you share copies of this book with someone, each time you inspire others with your story, each time you declare your amazingness, you create a ripple effect. You encourage others to discover and celebrate their own amazingness. You become a source of hope, strength, and a model of resilience.

YOU ARE AMAZING!

Your journey is just beginning. You have a mission ahead, to not only acknowledge your own amazingness but to spread this light, love, and empowerment to others.

YOU ARE AMAZING!

Open your heart to the world, share your story, and inspire those around you. Continue to grow, continue to shine, continue to be amazing. Because you are, indeed, amazing!

Sharing your truth can inspire the world. Your voice matters. You never know what you can do until you try.

So go out there, try, and remember, you are amazing!

ABOUT THE AUTHOR

Dr. Katherine Y. Brown strives to uplift and inspire others, fostering a belief in their own amazingness. She believes that "I Am Amazing" will serve as a catalyst for readers to uncover their own strength, resilience, and remarkable qualities. Katherine hopes readers will discover that being amazing doesn't rely on external factors or beliefs from other people. These are principles she instilled in her own children and hundreds of people she has mentored through the years.

Katherine is an inspiring mother to four children–Anthony D. Rodgers, Sydney Y. K. Brown, Irving D. Brown, and Robert D. Brown. Born and raised on the Southside of Chicago, her life journey is a testament to the strength and resilience she teaches in her books. In her childhood, she saw firsthand how hard—almost impossibly so at times—it was to rise above the unfortunate circumstances that were part of her everyday life. She vividly recalls memories of struggling with a lack of resources in her own community. Yet, she participated in everything her public school had to offer, instilling in her a deep desire to serve others.

A community leader for over three decades, Katherine has garnered recognition for her dedication to making a positive impact on her community. Her journey includes founding Learn CPR America, LLC, and the Dr. Katherine Y. Brown (KYB) Leadership Academy. She has trained over 300,000 people for free in CPR and has mentored over 250 leaders through KYB. Her training initiatives have enabled her to host KYB conferences in Costa Rica; Colombia, South America; Dubai; South Africa; and the Turks and Caicos Islands.

Some of her leadership and civic engagement includes Junior League; Jack and Jill of America, Inc. (Nashville Chapter Vice President 2022-2024); The Links, Inc.; Top Ladies of Distinction Inc.; Charms, Inc.; Iota Phi Lambda Sorority, Inc. (Southern Region Outstanding Business Woman of the Year 2023); and the National Coalition of 100 Black

Women.

She has also served as Parenting and Family Chair and a Faculty Member for the Maxwell Leadership Certified Team. She has traveled internationally teaching as a Coach with the John Maxwell Leadership Foundation, visiting locations such as Papua New Guinea, Panama, and the Dominican Republic. Her involvement further underscores her dedication to nurturing and guiding the next generation of leaders. Katherine now enjoys life in Nashville, Tennessee with her husband, four children, and two rescue dogs she affectionately refers to as her furbabies.